Grandchildren of the LAKOTA

THE WORLD'S CHILDREN

Grandchildren of the LAKOTA

LAVERA ROSE
PHOTOGRAPHS BY CHERYL WALSH BELLVILLE

Carolrhoda Books, Inc./Minneapolis

In memory of Kateri, Kevin, and Ivy. —LR
For Luke. —CWB

Text copyright © 1999 by LaVera Rose
Photographs copyright © 1999 by Cheryl Walsh Bellville
Additional photographs courtesy of: LaVera Rose, p.10 (left), and South
Dakota State Historical Society, Pierre, p. 35 (left).
Map on p. 7 by Laura Westlund © 1999 by Carolrhoda Books, Inc.

Carolrhoda Books, Inc. c/o The Lerner Publishing Group
241 First Avenue North, Minneapolis, MN 55401 U.S.A.

Website address: www.lernerbooks.com

LIBRARY OF CONGRESS CATALOGING-IN-PUBLICATION DATA

Rose, Lavera.
    Grandchildren of the Lakota / Lavera Rose ; photographs by Cheryl
Walsh Bellville.
        p. cm. — (The world's children)
    Includes index.
    Summary: Introduces the history, culture, and beliefs of the Lakota
Indians through a description of the lives of several children living on the
Rosebud Sioux reservation in South Dakota.
    ISBN 1–57505–279–2 (alk. paper)
    1. Dakota children—Social conditions—Juvenile literature.
2. Dakota Indians—Social life and customs—Juvenile literature.
3. Rosebud Indian Reservation (S.D.) — Social life and customs—Juvenile
literature. [1. Dakota Indians — Social life and customs. 2. Indians of
North America — South Dakota — Social life and customs.] I. Bellville,
Cheryl Walsh, ill. II. Title. III. Series: World's children (Minneapolis, Minn.)
E99.D1R67 1999
305.23–dc21   98-5307

Manufactured in the United States of America
1 2 3 4 5 6 – JR – 04 03 02 01 00 99

Author's Note

Have you ever noticed how sometimes the more things change, the more they stay the same? That is how I see Lakota culture. We may wear jeans and T-shirts instead of deer-hide clothes, drive cars instead of riding horses, and shop at stores instead of hunting *tataŋka* (bison)—but we are still uniquely Lakota.

I am a member of the Rosebud Sioux Tribe. I moved away from my home on the Rosebud Reservation to a town called Onida. My younger brother and sister have chosen to remain on the reservation. For me, my family represents some of the many different paths available to Lakota people. Those who stay on the reservation continue to learn more about our culture and language. Those of us who leave the reservation struggle to retain what we learned while we lived there. There are also those, like my granddaughter Brittany, who have never lived on a reservation. It is especially important to pass our culture and language on to Lakotas like Brittany who are growing up in urban settings far from their relatives.

Lakota people may be spread out across much of western South Dakota, but we are still bound together. We all face issues of housing, education, and economic conditions. Even more important, we share a common view of our world because of our Lakota values. It is our special view of the world around us that sets us apart from the non-Lakota community.

Lakota means friend or ally. It is the name of a group of American Indians commonly referred to as Sioux. The word Sioux describes a large group of people, the Oceti Šakowiŋ, or Seven Council Fires. Before Europeans came to America, the Oceti Šakowiŋ lived in the north central area of the United States. The Ojibway, enemies of the Oceti Šakowiŋ, called them *nadouessioux,* which means "little snakes."

French fur traders later shortened the word to Sioux. This large group of American Indians consists of three subgroups who speak similar languages: Lakota, Nakota, and Dakota.

Lakotas are divided into seven major subgroups: the Oglala, the Sichangu, the Oohenuŋpa, the Miniconju, the Itazipco, the Sihasapa, and the Huŋkpapa. There are five Lakota reservations in South Dakota and a small part of North Dakota.

Living in the southwest quarter of South Dakota are the Oglala and the Sichangu. The Oglala live on the Pine Ridge Reservation. Red Cloud and Crazy Horse were famous Oglala leaders. The Sichangu live on the Rosebud and Lower Brule reservations. Spotted Tail was a great leader of the Rosebud people, and Iron Nation was an early leader at Lower Brule.

Karlye's family is from the Cheyenne River Reservation, Josh's family is from the Lower Brule Reservation, and Brittany's family is from the Rosebud Reservation.

Located in the north central part of South Dakota along the Missouri River are the Cheyenne River and Standing Rock Reservations. The Oohenuŋpa, the Miniconju, the Itazipco, and the Sihasapa live on the Cheyenne River Reservation. Big Foot, Four Bears, Charger, and White Swan were important leaders of the Cheyenne River Agency people. The Huŋkpapa live on the Standing Rock Reservation, which lies in both North and South Dakota. Sitting Bull was a famous Huŋkpapa leader.

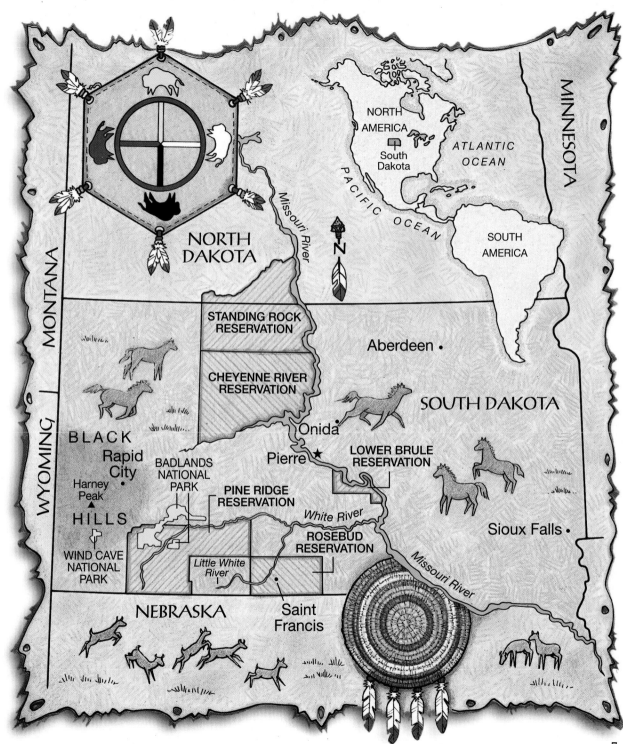

Before contact with Europeans in the 1600s, Lakotas lived a nomadic lifestyle. They followed herds of *tataŋka,* or bison, through their sacred homelands in western South Dakota—the Black Hills—and as far east as Wisconsin. When Europeans came to America, they settled on Indian lands. The Europeans thought that the Indians—with their different customs and religions—were inferior.

Tension grew between the two groups. Treaties, which are legal agreements between nations, were made between the United States and the Lakota to define land ownership. The Lakota fought for more than 100 years to keep their homelands. One treaty, written in 1868, gave ownership of the Black Hills to the Lakota.

On the banks of the Little Bighorn River in southern Montana, Lakotas fought General Custer to keep their lands.

Then in 1874, General George Armstrong Custer led an expedition onto Lakota land in the Black Hills and found gold. European-Americans (settlers from Europe) poured into the region. The Lakota fought for their land and defeated Custer's Seventh Cavalry in Montana—just west of the Black Hills—on the banks of the Little Bighorn River in 1876. But just one year later, the United States government used an invalid treaty to take the Black Hills as U.S. property.

During the 1880s, Lakotas were forced from their homes in the Black Hills onto smaller portions of land called reservations. They were no longer able to live their nomadic lifestyle. Their traditional customs and language were forbidden on the reservations. The *tiyoṡpaye,* or family unit, was torn apart when Indian children were sent away to boarding schools to learn the ways of European Americans. It was not until the 1970s that laws were passed to protect Lakota customs and most boarding schools were shut down.

These students from the Porcupine School on the Pine Ridge Reservation are on a field trip. Their teacher, Norma (center, in white shirt), shows them the Badlands, which can be seen in the background. She explains that Lakota land is essential to Lakota culture and must be protected for future generations.

Tye (left), *is Ardie* (middle) *and Nadine's* (right) *cousin, but they are brought up as one family and are treated equally by all the adults.*

Daniel stands with Elsie's sister Effie and his grandmother, Ina.

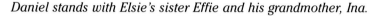

Daniel Yellow Hawk and his good friend Jay Roether live on the Rosebud Reservation. Daniel is 11 years old, and Jay is 10. Thirty years ago, before Daniel and Jay were born, Daniel's grandfather Tom adopted Jay's grandmother Elsie into his family. Although no formal paperwork was done, according to Lakota culture, Elsie became Tom's sister. They are not blood relatives, but they respect each other as though they were.

Kinship was and still is the tie that binds Lakota people. Lakotas place great importance on sharing with families and the community. Lakota people first work for the common good of their entire family, including grandparents, aunts, uncles, cousins, in-laws, and adopted family. Once the family's needs are met, they expand their sharing into the larger community.

Like their ancestors, Lakotas include many extended family members in their households. To make someone kin through adoption (as Elsie was) is a common practice among many Lakotas. Adoption increases the size of a *tiyošpaye* and promotes unity among different groups. After all, people don't usually go to war against their relatives!

Roger sits with his adopted daughter, Karlye Running Hawk. Like many Lakota families, Roger and his wife, Inez, have opened their home to include extended family members.

Daniel and his brother, John, live with their dad and grandparents. All of the adults share responsibility in raising Daniel and John. The Lakotas traditionally involved grandparents and other family members in child raising, and many Lakotas still do.

The Lakota word for children is *wakaŋyeja,* or sacred being. Children were the most important gift from Wakaŋtaŋka, the Great Spirit, to Lakota people. Children are the future of the Lakota Nation, so it is important to treat children with respect and kindness.

Above: *Zeno Little sings to his newborn nephew, Simon.* Right: *Lakota children are the future of the Lakota Nation.*

Above: *Karlye gets a hug from a relative.* Right: *Rose, a Lakota elder, passes on the Lakota language and culture to her grandchildren and their friends through stories she has learned from her own grandmother.*

Daniel's family is bilingual, which means they speak two languages. At home children learn Lakota from their grandparents, and at school they learn lessons in English. Learning the Lakota language is one way that Daniel and John learn about their Lakota culture.

Rose teaches her grandchildren about generosity. They discover that giving to others brings honor to both the giver and the receiver. One way to show generosity in Lakota culture is through an honoring ceremony, or giveaway. A giveaway may be held when a child is given a Lakota name, when someone graduates from high school or college, in thanks for an answered prayer, or when someone dies.

Through giveaways, children like Karlye and Kyla learn about the importance of giving and receiving.

Giveaways are a great responsibility for families. First the family makes or buys special gifts to give to the guests at the ceremony. Handmade pillows, quilts, and beadwork may be given to adults, while toys, candy, fruit, and soda pop are often given to children. On the day of the giveaway, the family prepares and serves a large meal. Throughout the day, the gifts are on display. Towards the end of the day, the gifts are passed out and given away. Long ago, horses were the most special gifts—but in the 1990s, people like to give handmade star quilts.

Brittany is seven years old. She lives in a town called Onida. She has never lived on a reservation, but she often visits her relatives at the Rosebud Reservation, where her mother is from. Two years ago, Brittany's younger sister, Ivy Rose, died. She was just three years old. Brittany and her family were shocked and saddened by Ivy Rose's death. They wanted the community to know that Ivy Rose is loved and greatly missed, so the family planned a memorial giveaway in her honor.

Over the winter, Brittany watched her grandmother sew baby quilts and pillows. Brittany's family bought many things that children would enjoy receiving: dolls, stuffed animals, cars, coloring books, trucks, crayons, and books. Each item was stored in a footlocker in Brittany's home.

Brittany's family decided not to have a traditional memorial for Ivy Rose. They wanted to help other non-reservation Lakotas who lived near them. The family chose to give most of their gifts to Lakota women and children at the Missouri Shores Domestic Violence Shelter near Onida, in Pierre. They also had a dinner at Brittany's cousin's house, on the Rosebud Reservation, in honor of Ivy Rose. After the meal, Auntie Inez treated the children to watermelon.

Inez passes out watermelon to children at a giveaway.

The Black Hills are foothills of the Rocky Mountains and rise 3,500 feet above the surrounding plains. Harney Peak rises 7,242 feet above sea level and is the highest point in North America east of the Rocky Mountains.

Brittany visits the Black Hills with her family a few times a year. She loves to look at the beautiful mountains, smell the wildflowers, and breathe in the fresh air. In the midst of the Black Hills is a place called Wind Cave. According to Lakota religion, the Lakota Nation was created inside Maka, or Mother Earth. Later, the Ikce Wicaśa, or common man, was led to the surface of Maka by the opening of Wind Cave.

Brittany's cousins Karlye and Helena join Britanny's family on their hike through the hills. Brittany's *uŋči,* or grandmother, talks about what their ancestors were doing in a time long past.

Helena and Karlye hike through the Black Hills.

16

Uŋči tells them about a small group of Lakotas who used to travel through the Black Hills during the spring months. These Lakotas patterned their movements after the motions of the sun. As the sun moved to certain sites, like Bear Butte and Harney Peak, the Lakotas held ceremonies there. At exactly the same time the Lakotas were performing ceremonies on Earth, spirits were performing the same ceremonies in the spirit world. The performance of these acts together in both worlds gave sacred power to the Lakota.

Brittany thinks about the story Uŋči has told her. It leaves her feeling strong and proud.

The Black Hills got their name from the dense ponderosa pine trees that cover the hills, making the hills appear black in color from a distance.

Below: *Kevin, John, Thomasina, Jeff, Kyla, and Allyssia like to spend time outside. When they visit the Badlands, they may see a prairie dog* (top right) *or a coyote* (bottom right).

Some areas in the Badlands are prairielike, while others are desertlike.

Kevin and Jeff Yellow Hawk are Daniel and John's cousins. The Yellow Hawk family owns land near the Badlands on the Pine Ridge Reservation, close to the southern Black Hills. The Badlands is an area of land that Native peoples call "bad land for crossing" because of its rugged terrain. Interesting rock formations and cliffs of various colors are a result of thousands of years of erosion and weathering.

When Kevin and Jeff visit the Badlands, they must be on the lookout for rattlesnakes that live in the desertlike area. Jackrabbits, prairie dogs, and coyotes also make their home in the Badlands.

There are places in the Badlands where little or nothing grows. The soil there is called gumbo, a heavy, red-colored clay that makes it hard for most plants to grow. But there are other areas in the Badlands where plants thrive. Wildflowers, sagebrush, yucca, and buffalo grass fill prairies for as far as the eye can see.

Above: *Some areas on Lakota reservations have up-to-date housing.*
Below left: *In other areas, the housing is run-down.*

Many Lakotas are very poor. They may live in low-quality housing in remote regions of the reservation without electricity or water. Some of these communities are so small that they do not have stores or post offices. The people who live there have to travel up to 30 miles for groceries. Another major concern on reservations is alcoholism. Yet despite such hardships, many Lakotas meet these challenges with great success.

For some, housing and the standard of living have improved on Lakota reservations. Up-to-date houses dot some prairie landscapes instead of log cabins and tipis. Some communities have built new hospitals, elementary schools, grocery stores, and tribal government offices.

Carol Jefferson

Since the early 1990s, tribal governments have sought to become less dependent on the federal government. Reservation governments are working hard to bring a better standard of living to their people. Both small and large businesses are encouraged to develop on reservations.

Maintaining order within the boundaries of each reservation is the responsibility of the tribal government. Tribal governments have their own sets of laws—they do not follow U.S. or state laws.

Tribal governments are, however, similar to the American government in many ways. Each reservation is governed by a council that is elected by the people for a term of two to four years. A tribal chairman, a vice-chairman, a secretary, and a treasurer are also elected. A council assists these officials in establishing laws that govern the people. A tribal law enforcement system also operates on each reservation. Tribal police officers, attorneys, and judges enforce the laws set up by the tribal council.

Carol Jefferson is a tribal policewoman who patrols the Rosebud Reservation. Carol lives on the reservation in a town called Saint Francis. It sits atop a ridge of canyons that are covered with pine trees. Carol takes long walks in the canyons to view the beautiful scenery.

Brittany and her friends run through a field on the outskirts of Saint Francis.

Since the 1970s, there have been significant changes in the way of life on Lakota reservations. One good change is the development of tribal schools and colleges. Here, students study Lakota culture and language.

It is important to teach these classes so that young people have a place—in addition to their home—to learn about their culture. Early Lakota culture relied on storytelling, or oral tradition, told by Lakota elders around an evening fire to teach history, customs, manners, and values. With the development of tribal schools, students can also learn this at school.

Jay, Jimmy, and Karlye live with their parents, Inez and Roger, at Saint Francis. The boys, along with their friend Allyssia, go to Saint Francis Indian School. Jay and Jimmy's father, Roger, drives a school bus. He must get up very early in the morning to pick up students who live outside St. Francis and bring them to school. Sometimes in winter, severe snowstorms prevent buses from traveling.

Saint Francis Indian School was once a boarding school, but it is no longer in use. A new Saint Francis Indian School has been built, at which children are taught Lakota culture and language, as well as U.S. history, science, and math.

Saint Francis Indian School has changed a lot in the past 20 years. Like most reservation schools, it was once a boarding school. Children stayed at school throughout the school year. They were not allowed to see their parents until school ended in the spring. Students were forbidden to speak their native language or practice their native customs. In addition, they were forced to learn the ways of European Americans.

Since the 1970s, Saint Francis Indian School has become a day school run by an elected school board. The emphasis is now on *preserving* Lakota culture and language rather than destroying it. Jay, Jimmy, and Allyssia learn about Lakota culture and history, in addition to learning U.S. history, science, and math.

Allyssia works on her assignment with a teacher's aide.

Wild roses (lower left), *wild plums* (left), *and coneflowers* (above) *can be found in prairies covering South Dakota.*

Grasses cover the prairies in western South Dakota. Coneflowers, sunflowers, soapweeds, pasqueflowers, bluebells, and wild roses are just a few of the flowering plants that bloom each year.

Inez enjoys harvesting native plants during the growing season. Karlye, Jay, and Jimmy like to help their mom pick wild turnips. They are taught to pull the turnip from the bottom of each clump of earth with their spades. In doing so, Maka (Mother Earth) is left undisturbed. Care is taken to leave some of the plants so that future generations may enjoy the vegetables, too.

Later, the children will braid the turnip stems together. Then they will hang the long cords of turnips to dry. The turnips can then be boiled in hot water with dried meat and dried corn to make a tasty soup.

Picking wild berries is great fun, too! Fresh berries—currants, chokecherries, wild plums, and buffalo berries—are picked from bushes that grow wild along the prairie hillsides. Jay likes to eat berries fresh from the bush. Jimmy prefers the berries cooked in a traditional pudding called *wojapi.* In the summer, Karlye helps her mother form mashed berries into patties, which are then dried in the hot sun.

Long ago, food was dried to prevent spoilage. By using this ancient method of preparing meat, vegetables, tea, and berries, Inez can feed her family many traditional foods. Some of the deer meat brought home last winter was eaten fresh, some was put in the freezer, and some was sliced very thin and then hung to dry. When dried, the meat is called p̊ap̊a saka, or pemmican. Once it is dried, Inez can pound the p̊ap̊a saka into shavings and mix it with dried berries and tallow to make a delicacy called *wasna*.

Left: *Jay digs for wild turnips while his friend Brandon plays nearby.* Above: *A wild turnip*

Before Lakotas were confined on reservations, they hunted *tataŋka*. *Tataŋka* provided food, clothing, and shelter for the people. The only *tataŋka* found in South Dakota in the late 20th century, however, are on reservation preserves and at Custer State Park in the Black Hills. Like the Lakota, the *tataŋka* survive—despite great changes in their environment. Even though they are not allowed to roam free, *tataŋka* remain an important part of Lakota culture.

Tataŋka *roam a nature preserve.*

In the winter, Roger takes Jay and Jimmy hunting. Instead of *tataŋka*, they hunt deer. The three walk along the top edge of the canyon, which was formed long ago by the Little White River as it wound its way through the Rosebud countryside. The scent of pine trees lingers in the fresh, crisp morning air. As Roger, Jay, and Jimmy walk, they look for signs of deer. If the hunt is successful, the family will have a supply of deer meat, or venison, for the winter.

Roger hunts with his sons, Jay and Jimmy.

Lakotas hunt mule deer for their meat, which is called venison.

Another activity Jay and Jimmy enjoy is fishing. They fish at all times of the year—even in the winter. They bundle up in several layers of clothing to protect themselves from the harsh winter temperatures. On an average day in January, it might be 16°F (–9°C). The boys take along a can of whole-kernel corn to use as bait. They cut a small hole in the ice, drop their line into the water, and wait for a fish to bite. When the boys get tired of waiting, they skate along the ice.

Jay baits a hook with corn (inset) *and then waits to catch a fish.*

Left: *Kevin and Jeff cool off in a river on a hot day.* Below: *Inez and Karlye search for wild mint along the roadside.*

In the summer, Kevin and Jeff often visit one of the small lakes near their home to fish for trout, catfish, and bass. Summer temperatures in South Dakota can get hot, but the average July temperature is about 74°F (23°C). To cool themselves on very hot days, Kevin and Jeff may jump into the water.

Inez and Karlye walk along the roadside to look for wild mint plants. When they get home, Inez bundles the mint they gathered and hangs it from the ceiling to dry. Later she will use the leaves to brew a delicious tea.

31

Inez does beadwork to decorate clothing for dancing.

Inez is making outfits for Jay, Jimmy, and Karlye to wear when they dance at powwows. She sews brightly colored glass beads onto leather for their moccasins. Karlye is learning to bead from her mother. One day she may sell her crafts at powwows and craft fairs.

Many Lakotas support their families from money they earn making and selling traditional handicrafts, such as quillwork and beadwork. Before Europeans introduced glass beads to the Lakota, they used dyed porcupine quills to decorate their clothing. In the 1990s, reservation governments set up programs to help Lakotas sell their handicrafts. Both quillwork and beadwork are popular items among tourists who visit South Dakota. Earrings, baseball caps, purses, and moccasins are sold in local stores and at craft fairs.

Inez (left) *and* *Jay* (below)

Karlye holds a hand drum decorated with tataŋka *and a medicine wheel. In Lakota religion, the medicine wheel is important because it shows the four colors that represent the directions of the earth, and it symbolizes the continuous circle of life.*

Jay's family practices Lakota religion. Like many other young Lakotas, Jay wants to learn the ways of his ancestors. These religious practices were once forbidden by the United States government. But thanks to the American Indian Religious Freedom Act of 1978, Lakotas can practice their traditional ceremonies without fear of punishment.

One such ceremony is the *wiwaŋyaŋk,* or sun dance. In this ceremony, participants offer Wakaŋtaŋka the greatest gift they have—their flesh and blood. The sun dance is held during the summer and lasts for four days. On those days, the dancers do not eat solid food but nourish themselves only with water.

The dancers move in a circle around and around and around. The circle represents our universe. The dancers dance to the beat of a round drum. As the participants dance, they pray hard for their personal prayers and the prayers of the entire Lakota Nation.

Family members and friends stay nearby to offer their support to the dancers and send their own prayers to Wakaŋtaŋka.

Jay's father, Roger, pledged to participate in the annual sun dance every year for four years. During the four years, Roger must live ac-cording to the teachings of the Sacred Pipe, the Lakota symbol of religious ritual. He must respect, honor, and help others.

One day, Jay will partici-pate in the sun dance him-self. Until then, he can learn about the ceremony from his father. Jay also helps with the preparations for the sun dance. He can gather wild sage, a plant that is used for physical and spiritual purifi-cation. Jay and his family also collect gifts and special foods for the honoring cere-mony that will be held in the fourth year of Roger's partici-pation in the sun dance.

Sage plays an important part in ceremonies and religion.

In the late 1800s or early 1900s, Standing Bear, a Miniconju Lakota, created this drawing on muslin that shows the sun dance.

Nadine (left), *who lives on the Pine Ridge Reservation, and her cousin Čaŋte Wašte Wiŋ* (right), *who lives in Minneapolis, Minnesota, get together at the Pine Ridge powwow.*

Many Lakotas have moved to nearby urban areas. Rapid City, Sioux Falls, Aberdeen, and Pierre are cities in South Dakota with large Lakota communities. Denver, Colorado, and Minneapolis, Minnesota, also have large Lakota communities. In these large cities, many Lakotas live near each other to be close to their people.

Čaŋte Wašte Wiŋ lives in Minneapolis. Her cousin Nadine lives on the Pine Ridge Reservation in South Dakota. The girls don't get to spend much time together. But each summer, both girls attend the Pine Ridge annual *wačipi,* or powwow, with their families.

Wačipis are social gatherings where people can get together to camp and visit in the summer months. It is a chance for young and old alike to meet friends and relatives. Like Pine Ridge, Rapid City, Minneapolis, Denver, and Sioux Falls each have an annual *wačipi* that attracts native people from many nations, including the Lakota. Non-Indians also enjoy these spectacular events.

By participating in the annual Pine Ridge *wačipi,* Čaŋte Wašte Wiŋ helps to keep Lakota customs alive. Even though she lives in a city, and not on a Lakota reservation, she can still learn about Lakota culture.

Minneapolis, Minnesota, is home to a large Lakota community.

Fancy shawl dancers are ready to begin their competition. At this powwow, they will compete for cash prizes.

On reservations throughout Indian country, *waċipis* are held each weekend all summer long. The gatherings last two to four days and may include naming ceremonies and giveaways. Dancers and singers travel from other reservations to compete for cash prizes.

Dancing has changed over the years. Years ago, Lakotas adorned themselves with feathers, hides, horns, teeth, or similar items borrowed from their winged and four-legged relatives. When they danced, they often copied the movements of the particular bird or animal whose features they wore.

In more recent years, dancers who practice this style of dance have been called traditional dancers. Men wear large circles of feathers called bustles on their backsides, and headgear called a roach, made of porcupine and deer hair, on their heads. Bells around their ankles chime with each step they take.

Women wear long deer-hide dresses with intricate beadwork covering the portion above the waist. The dancers move rhythmically up and down, circling the dancing men.

In addition to traditional dancing, other types of dances are performed at *wačipis:* fancy, fancy-shawl, grass, jingle-dress, and gourd dances. Fancy dancers wear brightly colored outfits and dance very fast to the beat of a drum. They look like brilliant flashes of color swirling through the dance arena.

These dancers are a blur of color.

Above: *These Lakota girls rest between dances.* Right: *Miss Teen Indian Day rides in the parade at Saint Francis.*

Jay, Jimmy, and Karlye like to attend Indian Day in Saint Francis each June on the Rosebud Reservation. This annual *wačipi* is similar to a county fair. There is usually a parade, a rodeo, a dance, a giveaway, and a softball tournament.

Karlye enjoys the parade. She watches the floats that carry special people—such as Miss Teen Indian and powwow royalty from other communities. Karlye can also ride horses, enjoy good food, and listen to music. At the *wačipi*, Jimmy plays softball. It is a very popular summer activity for young and old alike on most South Dakota reservations. A lively softball tournament can almost always be found at Saint Francis!

Left: *The Oglala Nation Powwow is a huge event. People from all over the country attend the* wačipi. Above: *At the Pine Ridge rodeo, world champion Howard Hunter* (second from left) *is presented with a quilt in his honor.*

The Oglala Nation Powwow is much larger than Indian Day. Held annually in August at Pine Ridge, the fair draws hundreds of spectators and participants. People from all over Pine Ridge, as well as other reservations, come to attend the fair, powwow, and rodeo. Carnivals and softball tournaments are also popular attractions. Indian world-champion saddle-bronc rider Howard Hunter is from Pine Ridge Reservation.

Daniel and John's father, Dean, as well as Kevin and Jeff's father, Tom, has a special interest in reservation fairs. They supply horses to local rodeos. Horses, like bison, are an important aspect of Lakota culture. Many Lakota people still consider themselves great horsemen. But instead of stealing horses from enemy nations, they prove their skills by competing in Indian rodeos. Dean and Tom travel the Indian rodeo circuit throughout the United States.

Sometimes the boys travel with their fathers from rodeo to rodeo. The boys like to watch the wild horse race, an event that Dean and Tom entered when they were younger. At the end of the summer, the National Indian Rodeo Finals are held. This exciting event is sometimes held in Rapid City, South Dakota.

Ina, Dean's mom, has land a few miles south of Saint Francis that she inherited from her parents. During the summer, Ina likes to work in the garden with her daughter-in-law, Julie, and granddaughters, Allyssia and Thomasine.

Daniel, John, Jeff, and Kevin like to ride their horses in the surrounding pastures over gently rolling hills. The younger children ride one of the many Shetland ponies from Dean and Tom's herd. The Dakota prairie is a great place for children to play with their dogs, too.

Above: *At the Pine Ridge rodeo, horsemen prove their skills.* Right: *T.D. Garnette gets ready to participate in the rodeo while his friends look on.*

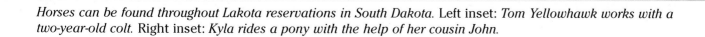

Horses can be found throughout Lakota reservations in South Dakota. Left inset: *Tom Yellowhawk works with a two-year-old colt.* Right inset: *Kyla rides a pony with the help of her cousin John.*

Brandon

Marissa Lopez

In 1980, the Supreme Court ruled that the Black Hills were unjustly taken from the Lakota by the U.S. government in 1877. The Supreme Court offered the Lakota money for the land. As of 1998, all but two Lakota bands have refused the money. Instead, many Lakotas continue to fight for their land in the Black Hills. So far, the U.S. has not agreed to return the Black Hills to the Lakota people.

The land, like the Lakota people, remains constant through many changes. Mining companies peel away layer after layer of earth to find more gold. Prairie grasses are tilled under as agricultural operations expand. Highways are built throughout Lakota country. Yet amid this technological growth, the sun still rises, birds still sing, wildflowers still bloom, deer multiply, and Bear Butte beckons us.

The changes we Lakota experience strengthen us. Brittany, Jay, Brandon, and Daniel go to movies, use computers, play basketball and volleyball, try to look cool, listen to rock and roll and country music, and go to school—just like other American children. At the same time, our Lakota traditions and values are our lifeline to our past.

When I look at my granddaughter Brittany I see the future of the Lakota people. My grandmother told me her story just as I have told my story to Brittany. One day, Brittany will pass her story on to her own grandchildren.

Pronunciation Guide

Čaŋte Wašte Wiŋ   KAHN-tay WAHS-tay win
Huŋkpapa   HUNK-pah-pah
Ikce Wicaša   ick-CHAY wee-CHAH-shah
Itazipco   ee-TAH-zeep-cho
Maka   mah-KAH
Miniconju   mee-nee-CON-joo
nadouessioux   nah-doo-sue
Oceti Šakowiŋ   oh-CHAY-tee shah-KOH-win
Oglala   og-LAH-lah
Oohenuŋpa   oh-OH-hey-NOON-pah
p̌ap̌a saka   BAH-bah SAH-kah
Sichangu   see-CHAHN-goo
Sihasapa   see-HAH-sah-pah
Sioux   SOO
tataŋka   tah-TAHN-kah
tiyošp̌aye   tee-YO-shbah-yae
uŋči   oon-CHEE
wačipi   wah-CHEE-pee
Wakaŋtaŋka   wah-KAHN-tahn-kah
wakaŋyeja   wah-KAHN-yae-jah
wasna   wah-SNAH
wiwaŋyaŋk   wee-WAHN-yunk
wojap̌i   WOH-jah-bee

Index